Sue L. Adkins

KWANZAA CELEBRATION

A Play In Two Acts With Music

KWANZAA CELEBRATION

Cover Painting by Frank Frazier II

ISBN 0-9672605-3-1

Copyright 2004 Cheudi Publishing

KWANZAA CELEBRATION

A Play In Two Acts With Music

By
Sue L. Adkins

ISBN 0-9672605-3-1
Cheudi Publishing, Plano, Texas 75094-0572

ROYALITY NOTE

The possession of this book (e-book or hard copy), without a written authorization first having been obtained from the publisher, confers no right or license, to professionals or amateurs, to produce the play, publicly or in private, for gain or charity. However, productions of this play are encouraged, and those who wish to present it may secure the necessary permission from Cheudi Publishing, Plano, Texas 75094, USA.

Professional producers are requested to apply to Cheudi Publishing for Royalty quotation.

This play may be presented by amateurs, upon payment to Cheudi Publishing of a royalty (to be determined) for each performance, one week before the date the play is to be given. The play is fully protected by copyright, and anyone presenting the play without the consent of Cheudi Publishing, will be liable to penalties provided by the copyright law.

Each time the play is produced, the name of the author must be carried in all publicity, advertising, fliers, and programmes.

Dedication

This play is dedicated to my husband Henry, who is the love of my life and the inspiration behind everything I do; and to my daughter, Angela, who acts as my motivator and editor. To my sons, Morgan and Cryston, who always encourage me. They are talented in their own right. Thanks and love to my mother Willie, an angel, who has gone from this life and remains in my heart; and to my brothers-in-law and my brother Cliff, a talented and gifted singer of the Gospel; to my sisters-in-law, especially to Chandra who has been a booster from the beginning. Thanks to all my aunts, uncles, my cousins, my nieces and nephews who keep me thinking and writing. You have all my love.

Acknowledgements

I want to thank you Ashira for encouraging me to write this play. It has been a beautiful learning experience for me. To those who read and perform this work, enjoy the words and songs, and commit the ideals and content to memory. It is my hope that this and other works about Kwanzaa will be performed on a regular basis. Thank your Dr. Maulana Karenga for formulating this amazing work and bringing it to the people. We are blessed because of it. This play can be adapted to fit various age groups by choosing to leave out or include segments or songs. Enjoy!

Note From The Author

Many people seek connection with their history, ancestors, and the country of their origin. For African Americans this has been a difficult task. Most have no connection with their ancient homeland. Some efforts have been made over the years to reach out to Africa and embrace the country and people. And there has been some measure of success. Dr. Maulana Karanga, an educator and political activist thought more was needed to strengthen and bridge the gap between Afro-Carribean, Latin, and African-Americans with the people of Africa. He focused on the similarities, customs, symbols, and food. From his research he created a cultural event built around the traditional time of harvest. With focus on specific principles, he encourages learning, discipline, and working together.

In 1966 Dr. Karanga revealed his work. It was established to help build a bridge between peoples; to strengthen, develop and move them towards excellence. He created a holiday and annual event to be handed down from generation to generation. "Kwanzaa Celebration" is a play which embraces Dr. Karanga's work. It focuses on a group of children at a community center that is hosting a Kwanzaa event. Tension and uncertainty develops over whether the event will go on as planned. The Swahili language is used to introduce the principles and symbols to build and strengthen people, families and communities. You are invited to learn and enjoy the celebration through the language, songs, dance, and stories which come together in a rich and vibrant message of oneness.

KWANZAA CELEBRATION
A Play In Two Acts With Music

By Sue L. Adkins

Act I
Scene I: *The Herman Ismus Holland Community Center prepares for the evening Kwanzaa Celebration*

Miss Ross: "Okay everybody! Let's hurry and finish, then get dressed!"

Minda: (*To Brett*) "Miss Ross looks worried." (Shrugs, both nod; continue working)

Director: "Everything okay Carol?"

Miss Ross: "Yes. Sure."

Director: "Good. We don't need *any* problems." *(Miss Ross nods. Gives weak smile)* "I let you talk me into this." (Sighs) "And I'm still not sure it was such a good idea."

Miss Ross: "It's important. And it *is* good. See how excited the kids are? I am too."

Director: "That's fine, but, we don't need problems. These parents are just starting to be okay letting their kids come here."

9

Miss Ross: "I know. Don't worry. Everything's under control." (*Kids enter*)

Director: "Let's hope it stays that way."

Miss Ross: "It will." (*Director exits. She claps, her hands, gets kid's attention*) "All right! Listen up! Today will be our first Kwanzaa Event here! (*All cheer*) "Okay! Listen! Your parents are coming, and I know they will love what you've done. Plus we get to eat all kinds of yummy food!" (*More cheers*)

Minda: "My parents are bringing something!"

Brett: "Mind too!"

Miss Ross: "Good!"

All: "I helped my Dad make a potato casserole! And I made green beans with my Mom!"

Miss Ross: "Sounds great. Okay. Finish decorating before our guests arrive. I'm putting Minda and Brett in charge!" (*To others*) "Everybody cooperate with them."

All: "Okay! Yes ma'am!"

Miss Ross: "All right! Let's get going!" (*Exits*)

All: "Yes Ma'am!" (*Minda and*

Brett step to the front of the group as Miss Ross exits)

Minda: "Okay everybody! Let's go!"

All: "Yeah! All right!

Song: "Come Join Together"

Brett: "Dannah! Can you help me move that table." (Pointing)

Dannah: "Uh-huh! Okay." (*Struggles to move table*) "Oh-h! This thing's heavy. Help!"

Minda: "Gail! Taylor! Help Dannah."

Gail &
Taylor: "All right! Okay!" (*Others come to help*)

Dannah: "Where does it go?"

Gail: (*Points*) "You remember! The middle of the room." *(Table's heavy; they rest. Others decorating, Shawn's tossing decorations)*

Helen: "Shawn! Put that down!"

Shawn: "I'm not hurting anything!" (Rips decoration) "Oops!"

Helen: "Look what you did!" (*Shawn drops it, gets another*)

Shawn: (*Yells, throws at Billy*) "Hey, Billy!" (*Laughing*)

Helen: "Minda! Look at Shawn and Billy!"

Minda: "Stop it guys! We've got work!"

Billy: "I didn't do anything! It's not me!"

Minda: "Stop playing and finish!"

Billy: "It's Shawn!"

Minda: (*Sighs*) "I'm telling Miss Ross! We gotta' get this done!"

Billy: "I'm working! Shawn's not!"

Dannah: (*Calls for help*) "Hey! Somebody help!"

Minda: (*Sighs*) "Now what! Oh no! You still don't have the table where it goes?

Taylor: "It's heavy!"

Roma: "Use your muscles!"

Helen: "What muscles?" (*Laughs*)

Taylor: "I need help!"

Minda: "Billy! Shawn! We need you!"

Billy: (*Drops decorations*) "I'm coming!
(*All but Shawn help*)

Minda: (*Sighs*) "Oomph! That's done!

Minda: "Helen! Get the mat and put it on the
table!"

Helen: "Okay!" (*Searches*)

Roma: "Mkeka!"

Helen: "We know!" (*Finds it*) "Here it is!"

Minda: "Good. Now let's finish. Come on
everybody!"

Song: "Karamu: The Feast"

Scene II : *(Hyla and Kim enter)*

Ms Ross: (*Enters*) "Minda? Why's everybody standing around? What's the trouble?"

Minda: "Shawn. He's not helping!"

Ms Ross: "I'll talk to him. Get everybody back to work!" (*Goes over to him*) "Shawn! We need your help!"

Shawn: "I *have* been helping! I'm just taking a little break."

Ms Ross: "Are you okay? You're not sick are you?"

Shawn: "No ma'am."

Ms Ross: "Okay, good! Rest time is over. We need you!" (*He stands up*)

Shawn: (*Whines*) "All right. What do you want me to do?"

Ms Ross: "Shawn what is it? What's wrong? This isn't like you."

Shawn: (*Yawns*) "I'm a little sleepy." (*Pause*) "My little sister had nightmares and kept me up all night. I had to get her water and take her to the bathroom three or four times."

Ms Ross: "Oh, I see." (*Smiles*) "Okay. This is what you need to do. Get moving and stay busy! That'll keep you awake!"

Shawn: (Yawns) "Excuse me. All right!"

Ms Ross: "Go wash your face. And just try to stay awake long enough to get through the program. Okay?"

Shawn: "Yes ma'am."

Ms Ross: "I know you're tired, but you'll make it."

Shawn: (*Yawns*) "I'm sorry."

Ms Ross: "That's all right." (*Shawn exits. Children continue working. To Roma*)
"Roma, are your parents coming?"

Roma: "Yes ma'am!"

Ms Ross: "Good. I think they'll like everything. It'll be fun!"(*To everybody*) "Okay everybody! Let's finish and get set! If you brought food make sure it's in the refrigerator."

Gail: "My Mom's bringing something when she comes."

All: "Mine too!

Ms Ross: "That's fine. All right everybody! Let's go!" (*Exits*)

Minda: "Back to work everybody!" (*Shawn enter, singing starts*)

Song Refrain: "Come Join Together"

(Minda begins singing, all join in, continue decorating - streamers, balloons, the Seven Principles Poster, Kwanzaa Banner, other decorations)

Minda: "This looks good. But something's missing."

All: "What? Everything's done! That's all, except for food. It looks fine!"

Minda: "Oh! I know! Kanara!"

Dannah: "Kanara?"

Taylor: "Oh yeah. That's important!"

Billy: "Kanara: The candleholder."

Gail: "And the Seven Candles: Mishumaa Saba."

Dannah: "Why do we need seven?"

Billy: "Because Mishumaa Saba, the Seven Candles, stands for Nguzo Saba - Seven Principles."

Dannah: "What?"

Brett: "He missed coming that day." (*Laughs*) "Hey! Let's explain it to him!"

All: "Yeah! Okay!"

Song: "Kanara - Candleholder"

Dannah: (*Hums the tune and repeats the words*) "Kanara, Candleholder. Mishuma Saba; Nguzo Saba, Seven Principles. Oh! I get it!" (*Sings, hums, helps finish work. Hyla and Kim enter*)

Scene III

Hyla: "Is Mommie coming?"

Kim: "Hyla you know she said she wasn't."

Hyla: "But she's got too."

Kim: "You heard her. She's not coming!"

Hyla: "Oh! But she needs to be here!"

Kim: "I *told* her. She said it was too close to Thanksgiving and Christmas. And she's got no time or energy for another holiday."

Hyla: "It's not fair." (*Pause*) "I don't care! I'm staying!"

Kim: "What? You can't! We have to leave right after we help decorate."

Hyla: "I'm staying for the whole thing! Miss Ross gave me a part. It's important! And I'm staying!"

Kim: "Hyla! Mommie told you to tell Miss Ross you couldn't do it!"

Hyla: "I didn't want to."

Kim: "Well you'd better tell her. Roma's doing my part. Mommie said for us to come home. Why didn't you tell Miss Ross we had to leave?"

Hyla: "Why didn't you?" (*Pause*) "I thought Mommie would change her mind."

Kim: "Mommie *never* changes her mind. And I

did talk to her." (*Pause. Sighs*) "You gotta' tell Miss Ross you can't do it so she can get somebody else! I can't believe you! It's probably too late to find anybody now!"

Hyla: "Oh-h, it's not fair! What did you tell Momma about Kwanzaa anyway?"

Kim: "You know. That it's for families to celebrate culture and tradition." (*Irritated*) "I told her we get to cook, and eat food we fix, and about the gifts."

Hyla: (*Interrupts*) "Oh no! That's why we can't stay! Now she won't let us do *anything* next year! Why did you have to mention presents? Mommie didn't hear you say we *made* them. She just heard '*gifts!*' To her that meant one thing."

Both: **"MONEY!"** (They nod)

Kim: "Just be glad we get to do this much."

Hyla: (Pleads) "Oh! Kim! Call Mommie back and ask; no *beg* her to let us stay!"

Kim: "No!"

Hyla: Tell her we've got to stay! A-and, that we're doing something special, so she needs to be here.

Tell her it starts at 6. And she won't have to bring anything." (*Begging*) "Please Kim! Tell her we **need** to stay! It's important!"

Kim: "Hyla it's no use."

Hyla: (*Begging*) "Kim, pleas-se talk to her!"

Kim: "Oh, all right! But it won't help."

Hyla: (*Sighs*) "Thanks Kim!" (*Hugs her*) "You're my favorite sister!"

Kim: "I'm your *only* sister."

Hyla: "She'll listen to you. Tell her to come! And she can bring food!"

Kim: "You said she didn't have to bring... Oh, I'll try! But don't expect miracles." (*Ms Ross enters*)

Hyla: "Do it Kim! Get her to let us stay. And tell her everything I said."

Kim: "Okay. I'll try."

Ms Ross: "Hyla! Kim! Is your Mom coming?

Kim: "I don't know."

Ms Ross: "Didn't you tell her about it?"

Hyla: "Yes ma'am." (*Kim shrugs, pleading look at Hyla, Her eyes urge her to tell Miss Ross the truth. Hyla shrugs. Exits*)

Ms Ross: (*To Kim*) "I hope she makes it."

Kim: "Me too." (*Exits*)

Ms Ross: (*Looks around*) "Oh-o-o, it looks good in here! Is everybody ready?"

All: "Uh-huh; almost!"

Ms Ross: "Okay, finish up and get in your costumes! Everybody knows their part."

All: "Yes! Un-huh! We do!"

Ms Ross: "Great! Get going and do a quick run-through in you mind. I'll be back!" (*Exits*)

Scene IV: (*Kim and Hyla enters. She whispers to Kim*)

Hyla: "Well?

Kim: "Well what?"

Hyla: "What did she say?"

Kim: "She said, come home!"

Hyla: "Why can't we do this?" (*Crying*)

Kim: "I don't know."

Hyla: (*Whining*) "I want to do my part!" (*Gail comes over*) "If she only knew about it she'd want us to stay. And she'd come too."

Kim: "Hyla, stop it! Let's just help and leave!"

Hyla: "No!" (*Stomps off*)

Gail: "What's the matter with Hyla?"

Kim: "She wants to stay and do the play, but our Mother said no." (*Shrugs. Taylor crosses, hands her decorations. All get busy*)

Dannah: (*Interrupts*) "What about this corn?"

Roma: (*Annoyed*) "Don't you know anything? Put it on that table! And it's called Muhindi (*Moo heen dee*). It represents children." (*Shakes her head in disbelief*)

Dannah: "Oh. What about this?"

Roma: "Kikombe Cha Umoja (*Kee Kom Bay Cha Oo mo jah*): a wooden cup. That's the symbol of

Unity. It's used in the Libation: Tambiko
Ceremony."

Dannah: "Oh-h! I'll never learn all this stuff!
Why can't we just call things by the names *we* know
instead of African names?"

Taylor: "Because this is a special time. And we
use words from the Swalihli language."

Dannah "Swalihli?"

Gail: "Yes-s-s."

Dannah: "I always wanted to learn another
language. But I thought it would be French or
Spanish."

Minda: "Those are good languages too. And so is
English." (*Dannah nods agreeing*)

Taylor: "But why not learn even more."

Dannah: "I don't think I'm that smart."

Roma: "That's got nothing to do with anything. If
you had been born and raised in a part of Africa
where that was the language, you'd be speaking it
with no problem, right?"

Dannah: (*Shrugs*) "I-I guess."

Brett: "So why not learn it? You can."

Billy: "Most people in other countries speak more than one language. A lot speak English too. And they're no smarter than any of us."

Dannah: (*Smiles*) "Oh, yeah."

Minda: "Kwanzaa is about linking our life, times, and people in America with the past in Africa."

Dannah: "Oh-h-h!"

Billy: "And then you build on that."

Taylor: "We need to know about our past, the language and a lot more."

Dannah: "I see."

Minda: "This way we can do it and have fun too!"

Taylor: "We get to wear African clothes."

Roma: "And fix our hair in African styles. You could wrap or braid your hair; or just wear it like you always do."

Dannah: "Yeah, cause I don't know how to braid."

Billy: "Somebody can show you."

Dannah: "Okay!" (*Kim and others enter*)

Kim: (*To Minda*) "Have you seen Hyla?"

Minda: "No."

Roma: "I think I saw her in one of the classrooms." (*Ms Ross enters*) "She looked sad."

Gail: "Yeah. She is."

Roma: "What's wrong?"

Gail: "Hyla and Kim want to stay for Kwanzaa, but their mom told them to come home after they help decorate."

Ms Ross: "You're not staying?"

Kim: "No ma'am."

All: "What? Why not? Who's doing your parts?"

Ms Ross: "Kim!" (*Director enters*) "You

and Hyla have parts in the ceremony!"

Kim: "Yes ma'am, I know. But somebody else has to do 'em."

Ms Ross: "Why didn't you tell me you couldn't stay?"

Kim: "We thought Mommie would change her mind."

Ms Ross: "Why doesn't your mom want you to stay?"

Kim: "She thinks Kwanzaa is just about money and buying presents and stuff. She said we already have Christmas."

Ms Ross: "I can understand that she doesn't want another reason to spend money; but did you tell her that's not what Kwanzaa's about?"

Kim: "I tried. But she didn't want to hear it."

Ms Ross: (*Sighs*) "Well, maybe I could talk to her."

Kim: (*Pause*) "I guess so. It might help."

Ms Ross: "I'll call to invite her and ask if you and Hyla can stay and do your parts. Okay?"

Kim: (*Sighs*) "Thanks Miss Ross."

Director: "I knew it! I knew this would cause problems."

Ms Ross: "There's no problem."

Director: "We didn't need to do this! These parents are not going to support it. They don't understand. I don't even understand!"

Ms Ross: "There's nothing *to* understand. Except that it's good for the children, parents; and for all of us!"

Director: "I don't see how! It's just an added burden." (*Sighs*) "Maybe we shouldn't do it!"

Ms Ross: "You can't shut it down before we even get started!"

Director: "I can and I will. Look, I don't want to stop it. But I may have to. This is a city sponsored center and program. And we don't need trouble."

Ms Ross: "Trouble? This is good and important! Our families need this. And I know you don't understand it now but…"

Director: "You're right I don't. Our program is in place. And this is just something somebody made up anyway."

Ms Ross: "That's how traditions start! It's from ideas and thoughts to encourage and build up the people and community. That's what this is about!"

Director: (Sighs) "Oh, I don't know."

Ms Ross: "Give it a chance! Give *them* a chance!"

Director: "I want to. But we don't need problems. People are watching us. Some think Centers like ours is a waste of money. So if we do this it's got to be right!"

Ms Ross: "Of course! But we know it's needed! These kids are ready! Their parents and everybody will understand in time."

Director: "But it looks like we have a problem."

Ms Ross: "It's nothing we can't handle."

Director: "Well make sure. Or this could be the

first and last Kwanzaa we have here. Take care of things!"

Ms Ross: "I will." (*Director Exits*) "All right!
Listen everybody! Hurry! Finish and get into
costumes."

All: "All right! Okay Miss Ross!"

Ms Ross: "Kim! Find Hyla. Tell her I'll
talk with your mom." (*Kim nods and exits*)
"Okay everybody! We don't have
Much time! Let's go!"

All: "All right! Yes Ma'am!"

(Miss Ross exits)

          Song: "Maulana Karenga"

          Act II

Scene I: Ms Ross enters

Ms Ross: (*Children enter in Costumes. To
Brett*) "Where are Kim and Hyla?"

Brett: *(Shrugs)* "I don't know.
I think they're getting dressed."

Ms Ross: "Oh, good."

Marla: "Miss Ross?"

Ms Ross: "Yes Marla? What is it?"

Marla: "Will this be a long celebration?"

Ms Ross: "I don't think so. Why?"

Marla: "Because my little brother's coming and he can't stay up too late."

Ms Ross: "No Marla, we'll be out at a reasonable time. I'm sure he'll do fine."

Marla: "Good, cause he gets fussy if he's not in bed on time."

Ms Ross: "I think he'll be all right." (*To children*) "Okay. Listen everybody! Remember. This is a celebration! So let's have fun. Enjoy it while we teach and learn. Is everybody ready?"

All: "Yes Ma'am!"

Ms Ross: "Okay! Great! We start in twenty minutes." (*Kim enters*) "Oh! Kim! I called your mom."

Kim: "What did she say?"

Ms Ross: "It was tough, but you and Hyla can stay."

Kim: (*Sighs with relief*) "Oh, good!" *(Pause)* "Is she coming?"

Ms Ross: "She didn't say. But I told her you both have important parts, and that I'd bring you home when it's over. Tell Hyla it's time."

Kim: "I can't find her."

Ms Ross: "What? Did you look in the classrooms?"

Kim: "Yes ma'am!"

Ms Ross: "What about the kitchen?"

Kim: (*Nods*) "She was pretty mad."

Ms Ross: "I hope she didn't leave!"

Kim: "No. She's hiding until time for her part."

Ms Ross: "I think you're right. But we need to look for her. *(To others)* "Everybody, I need your help!"

All: "Yes ma'am!"

Ms Ross: "Hyla's missing!"

All: "Missing? Where is she! Did she leave?"

Ms Ross: "We don't know. We'll work in teams and search the building. Check every room. Your parents will be here soon. You've got ten minutes, and then everybody get in place!"

All: "Yes Ma'am, all right!" (Kid exit)

Ms Ross: "Kim! Get dressed!"

Kim: "Yes Ma'am."

Ms Ross: "We'll find her."

Kim: "She'll be here at just the right time." (Exits. Minda enters in costume)

Ms Ross: "Minda! Stay here and welcome the parents. Make sure they get seated."

Minda: "Okay."

Ms Ross: "Oh!   And show the drummers where to set up."

Minda: "Yes ma'am." (Ms Ross exits)

Children: *(Enter. Greet parents)* "Habari
Gani? What is the Day?"

All: "Kuumba! Creativity!"

(Audience is greeted as the parents)

*(Drummers enter. Minda point them to setup space.
More children enter, take places. Ms Ross greets
parents)*

Ms Ross: "Kukaribisha! Welcome
Parents, families and friends. This is our
Center's first Kwanzaa Celebration.
Thank you for coming to join us.
Kwanzaa is based on ancient African Festivals and
customs. 'Watoto:' Your children, will
speak and sing in Swahili, an East African
language. Kwanzaa combines Afro-Caribbean,
Afro-Latin, and African-American customs and
ways. All we do, say and think, can help build
our community.

We give our children precious gifts of belief,
trust in themselves; respect and strong will
to grow as healthy productive citizens.
Look around the room and enjoy the wonderful
symbols of a people. Everything was done by *your*
children. Thank you for coming!"

(Drums/Ngoma, begins, signals start of celebration)

Song: "Habari Gani? What is the Day?"

(Children gather around Symbols of Kwanzaa on Kente cloth covered table)

Ms Ross: *(Whispers)* "Kim! Did you find Hyla?" *(Kim shrugs, shakes head no)*

Kim: "I couldn't find her!"

Ms Ross: *(Whispers)* "Let's go on. I'll keep looking." *(Kim nods, steps forward. Drums continue. Miss Ross exits. Kim picks up basket of fruits/vegetable. Drumming stops)*

Kim: "Mazao! *(Mah zah o)*: Straw basket. Filled with Vegetables and Fruits: Symbols of our roots: Bounty of our labor!" *(Points to place mat)*

"Mkeka! *(Mm kee kah)*: The Place mat. Symbol of the foundation of our traditions and history." *(Sits basket on the place mat. Points to candleholder.* "Kinara! *(Kah nah rah)*: The Candleholder, made of wood. It holds Mishumaa Saba! *(Mee shoo mah Sah bah)*: Seven candles: Symbol of our ancestors." *(She points)* "Muhindi! *(Moo heen dee)*,

Ears of Corn: Symbol of our Children.
Zawadi! (*Zah wah dee*): Gifts made by
Hand. Books which stand for knowledge
are treasured gifts."

*(Drums begin. Brett steps forward, Kim moves back
with the group)*

Brett: "Libation! (*Tambika*) is the pouring
of water on the ground. A Symbol of Respect for
the Ancestors. Please Raise the cup of Unity that
pulls us together." (*Picks up cup or goblet*)
Kikombe Cha Umoja Kee Kom Bay Cha Oo Mo
Jah: The Cup! Symbol of Unity and Oneness!" (*He
lifts it to the North*) "To the North Wind! Iba
Olodumare - I respect the Creator!" (Lifts
it to the East) "To the East Wind! Iba Orisha –
I Respect the Deified Ancestors!" (*Lifts it to
the South*) "To the South Wind! Iba Baba Mi
Ali Iya Mi Lai Lai - I Respect All My
Grandmothers and Grandfathers Back To The
Beginning! To the West Wind! Iba Bab Mi Ati
 Iya Mi - I Respect My Mother And My Father! Iba
Orimi! I Respect The Spirit of God In Me!
Iba Omoni! I Respect The Children Who
Are Coming!" (*Brett steps back and joins
the group. Roma steps forward to Sing and
 teach a song)*

Roma: "Listen to my Song, and Sing along with me!"

Song: "Kwanzaa Symbols"

(Drum Beats for lighting of the Candles)

Gail: "Mishumaa Saba! (*Mee Shoo Mah Sah Bah*). Seven Candles. We light the First Candle for the First Day and on through the Seven days of Kwanzaa. This is the Sixth day of Kwanzaa." (*She lights the middle black candle, and a red, a green, a second red, and green, and a third red candle as the Drum beat get louder*)

Song: "Seven Candles"

Taylor: "The Nguzo Saba! *Seven Kwanzaa Principles*; Everyone please repeat the Principles after me!"

Taylor: "Umoja! (*Oo mo jah*) Unity!"

All: "Umoja! Unity!"

Taylor: "Kujichagulia! (*Koo Gee Chah Goo Lee Ah*) Self-Determination!"

All: "Kujichagulia! Self-Determination!"

Taylor: "Ujima! (*Oo Jee Mah*)
Collective Work & Responsibility!"

All: "Ujima! Collective Work & Responsibility!"

Taylor: "Ujamaa! (*Oo Jah Mah*)! Co-operative Economics!"

All: "Ujamaa! Co-operative Economics!"

Taylor: "Nia! (*Nee Ah*) Purpose!"

All: "Nia! Purpose!"

Taylor: "Kuumba! (*Koo Oom Bah*) Creativity!"

All: "Kuumba! Creativity!"

Taylor: "Imani! (*Ee Mah Nee*) Faith!"

All: "Imani! Faith!"

Taylor: "Today is the sixth day of Kwanzaa. The Principal is Kuumba (*Koo-Oom-Bah*) Creativity! Give your all in whatever you do. Use the gifts you have within to always make things better than how you found them."

Song: "Seven Principles"

(Kim steps forward, lifts Unity Cup, pases it around to all who make gesture of drinking)

Kim: (*Drum Beats*) "Kikombe Cha Umoja! The Unity Cup. Pass it around for each one to drink. The Symbol of Unity and Harmony of the gathering. Everyone! Repeat after me! "Harambee! Let's pull together! "Harambee! Harambee!" (*Repeat Seven Times! Drums continue, children form circle. Miss Ross directs parents to come and form a circle around the children*)

Ms Ross: "Parents join us!" (*Choose equal number parents as children in the circle. Each stands behind a child. She hands each a gift to give to a child*) "Form a circle around the children as we celebrate with Zawadi!" (*Zah Wah Dee*) "Gifts we have made. As a gift is given to a child, parents speak the name of a Hero or Heroine!" (*She hands gift to a parent who gives it to the child she or he stands behind. This continues all around the circle*)

Song: "Zawadi The Gift"

Minda: (*Story Teller Steps Forward,
gives piercing call. All sit and listens. Minda
claps her hands to begins*) "Sit! Listen! Time
for a story!" (*Parents return to the audience*)
"Everyday of the seven days of
Kwanzaa, a story should be told. Seven days of
Kwanzaa! And Seven Stories!"
(*She claps her hands again, goes and sits. Drums
begin, with softer beat. The story is told in word and
dance. Hyla steps out in costume; hugs Kim and
gets in position. She is the character Einja. As the
story is told she will dance as other characters move
into place*)

Storyteller: *(Shakes her beads as drums
play)*
  "Our story begins! **Einja's Beautiful Song**

(*Einja walks away from village and enters a forest of
lush vegetation*)

A bright sun sparkling morning Einja rushed
out to play. She daydreams, walks, and skips
along the way. A butterfly flutters, maybe a bee,
a tiny horsefly, bug or flea. It stops at a bud,
jumps, sails over the mud; lands on a petal

without a thud; drinks nectar from each flower.
Oh Wow! That's insect power!
(Einja sees plants, flower, insects; watches butterfly)

It floats, spins, twirls; makes a loop-de-loop of
swirls, Poof! Vanishes then re-appears. Hooray!"
she cheers. There hanging in mid-air, wings
aflutter; woe, a faint stutter. Then gone again,
Oh brother!

*(Einja's runs to catch the butterfly, she sneezes,
arms outstretched, eyes wide)*

Einja runs fast hoping to catch the thing posing in
the breeze; and if it's caught, not hold too tight,
and squeeze. Zip! It was gone again quick as a
sneeze. Ah-chew!

(Bird Sound) "Aw!" she said. *(Bird Sound)*
"Oh!"
*(Einja hears beautiful sounds. She trips, falls, is
tangled in plant, gets hits on the head; she sneezes)*

She tripped, fell, got tangled in a vine. *(Doing)*
Bopped on the head, a little chill; "Oomph!" Not
feeling so fine.

(Bird sound) "What *is* that?" *(Bird sound)*
"There!" With a huge grin so big her mouth got
sore, she followed that sound to the ocean shore,

until she came to where she had never been before.
(*Einja hears bird sounds, grins, heads toward sound and the ocean*)

There sat a bird on a limb in the sea, preening, singing; making his plea. *(Bird sound)* **What if** *she* **could make a sound like that? Not a laugh, no, but better than what comes from a gnat.**
(Gnat sound)

(*Bird perched on branch in the Ocean. Einja stands watching*)

A woman appears, holding a water pot cradled so dear. She wades into the ocean clear; fills the pot then comes over near. "Hello! I love to hear the bird's singing. Don't you?" she said. "Yes!" Einja said wanting to know more. "Oh! We never met before," The woman said.

"No. But I wish I could make *that* **sound," Einja said, pointing to the bird. "Then you must! For deep inside you it can be found!" the woman said. "Super! The best! But will I have to live in a nest?" Einja said. The woman smiled, shook her head, and sat down to rest.**

In time, off the bird flew. And with no more talk the quiet grew. The woman looked deep into Einja's eyes then picked up her water pot, waved goodbye, and headed off to where she was not.

(Einja and woman with water pot sit looking at bird in the Ocean)

Einja rushed home anxious to tell about her day. She saw sister Jada and friend Summa at play. They heard mother's call, "Einja! Jada! Come to dinner all!"

(Family at dinner table)

With a feast on the table, and fresh berries to eat; father's tales of humpback whales made the day complete. Oh how neat! Jada's laugh filled the room like flowers spilling in bloom.

Einja," Mother said. "Tell us about your day. When she opened her mouth to say, out came a strange sound. "Oh! What? Turn around!" Mother said. "Talk plain!" But Einja couldn't, though she tried to explain.

(Einja opens her mouth, makes bird sounds. All look surprised)

"Speak Einja!" *(Bird Sounds)* "No! Not sounds that come from a beak!" Father said. He tried to stay calm, not get mad, or weak; and think what to do about the gawks and squawks?"

So he gathered pieces of charcoal for her to write upon the ground and draw; make pictures of what she saw; and to give some clue of what, when, where, and who. But Einja didn't understand what to do.

(Father gathers pieces of rocks, huge leaves, animal hides, stone chalk)

Father was mad, furious and sad. *(Bird Sound)* "Oh! My Word! Again sounds of a silly ole bird," he said. "My word!" mother said with a cackle, scared of what they must tackle. Jada looked muddled and befuddled. But Einja liked what she had and was glad.
(Family looks at Einja, with sad, surprised, angry faces)

All beg her to talk, as they fidget and balk, but again came the sound. Sh-h-oom! It moved around the room. Foo-oom! Bird sounds magic and loose, Zoom like a runaway caboose. All cried "Boo-Hoo!" Every single one did too!
(Father sends Jada for the doctor)

43

(Bird Sound) **"Bah! That's bad!" Father said. "He couldn't think, till something inside him went 'CLINK!' "Oh! Jada! Go! Get the doctor! "Hurry child! Run quick! Say that your sister is sick!"**

(Jada and Doctor return. Father pacing, looks worried)

When the Doctor and Jada got back, father was fumbling and mumbling. "Despicable! Ickible," he said in a chanting rant. "Is your wife sick? Taken to bed rather quick?" Doctor said. "No!" Father said. "It's Einja, our child, once mild, who is now changed to wild."

(Mother sits rocking, crying, pointing Doctor to Einja's room)

Inside mother rocks, cries, wails, and shakes her head, her face a flush of red. She points to the room where her child lay in bed. "See where her disobedience led! Help my child! She pled.

(Einja sits on her bed as Doctor examines her head, hands, feet, eyes, ears)

(Family peeks in room looking scared, nervous)

Doctor went in and checked her heart. "H-m-m-m, okay! Eyes: Clear! Ears: Hello! Yes-s-s!

The child moves and hears! Hands and feet: Uh-huh! Mother! Father! Jada! Come here!" The family peeked in; then entered that trio with none among them the hero.

"Why did you rush me here? Everything's all clear!" Doctor said. "No. Let *her* talk! Listen and hear," father said. "Come, come! Speak! Okay?" he said. "We can't wait all day!" Doctor said.

(Doctor and family in Einja's room; All look sad, scared and worried)

She opened her mouth and out leaped, "Peep, Peep!" Doctor gasped. "Tell us more! Like before," Father said. "S-sq-aw-k!" she said. "Oh!" Doctor could only gulp and gawk. "Terrible! Awful!" Mother cried. "What a mess!" Doctor said, "Oh, the stress!"

(Doctor, Family gasp, look surprised, sad, confused)

Father was angry. Mother stood at his side. Jada looked for a place to hide. Doctor had to think. "Aw-w!" he said. Then things came together in a blink. "To change this, go back to the land of bird's "Coo-Coo! That place known to me and a

few others too-too! Oh!" Doctor said with a
stutter. "Go back to that spot at the same time,"
he said. "Tomorrow then," father said his face
now sour as a lime.

*(Father is angry; mother's sad; Jada looks
confused)*

There was little time to think. Night passed in a
blink. The next day they left in a hurry, back to
that distant place all did scurry.

*(Family walks to forest; the ocean and clearing seen
beyond)*

Walking through a tangled, wooded net, near the
clearing she left to go alone to where she must get.
That bird forlorn flew back looking sad and
worn. He stretched his neck to sing, but no sound
could it bring. Nothing came from the Wren. So
Einja made the sound for him right then.
(Einja's Bird Sound)

*(Family in the woods near the clearing, hug, wave
goodbye to Einja, who goes on alone) (Sad bird sits
on limb in the sea, beak open; as Einja sings)*

Again the woman appeared on the shore. She
filled her water pot once more. "Oh! It's you!
Had enough time with the bird sounds?" she said.

Einja nodded. "Be sure! Once it goes you can never again make the sweet blend. That will be the end," She said. Einja paused then gave a nod. "It's done then!" The woman said. When Einja opened her mouth to sing, out came, "Hello! Oh!"

(Einja sits on shore as woman appears with water pot)

(Einja's mouth's open, she has a strange look on her face)

"Hello!" she said again. "Oh! No!" Einja didn't think it would happen so fast. Now it was gone forever. Would it return? No, never. Her family came running. "I'm me again!" She said. They all hugged, smiled, and cried with joy. "Your voice is back! Not sounds that annoy," father said.

(Family rushes from the forest to greet Einja; hugs, smiles)

"We never want to lose any part of you again!" Mother said. "We love how you talk, laugh, walk; and fun stories of things you do. Always be who you are too," they said. "I will," Einja said.

"Ready?" mother said. Einja looked back. The woman and bird were gone. But she had her family and was not alone. "Yes!" she said. "Good. Let's go home," father said. Now she liked herself

**how she was, just so. And you should too. Yes!
Now everybody's ready and set to go!**
(Family heads home)

The End

Storyteller: *(Shakes her beads and claps her hands.)*
"That is the end of my story on the sixth story of Kwanzaa. There are seven stories to tell; one for each of the seven days of Kwanzaa. There are Seven Candles of Kwanzaa and Seven Stories." *(She shakes her beads and claps her hands again)* "The Karama is ready! Let us feast!"

Miss Ross: *(She and Director Step forward)* "Asante! Asante Sana! Thank you! We are honored with your presence!"
(Sees Kim and Hyla's mother, motions her to join them. Kim and Hyla hug her)

Director: "You did it! This was a beautiful program!"

Miss Ross: "Yes. The children did a great job. And I think the parents enjoyed it and learned a lot too."

Director: "I think you're right! I learned something too! This will to be a good thing to do every year!"

Miss Ross: "Yes it will!" *(To parents/audience)* "Thank you to all our parents for being here! Asante!"

Director: "Asante! Asante Sana!"

Song: "Kwanzaa Means First Fruit"

End

Production Notes

Kwanzaa Celebration can be adapted and performed by elementary, middle and high school students.

<u>Set</u>: The play is set in a neighborhood community center. Students are decorating and preparing to hold a Kwanzaa Celebration. It is the sixth day of Kwanzaa.

<u>Characters</u>:
Center Director, Miss Ross
Minda/ Woman with water pot
Bret/Bird
Danah/girl
Gail/Storyteller
Bill/Father
Helen/Einj and Jada's Mother
Shawn/Doctor
Taylor/Boy
Roma/Girl
Kim/Jada
Hyla/Einja
Marla/Summa
Drumers

Props:

Banners: (Welcome to Kwanzaa Celebration; Map of Africa. Seven Principles. Decorations; Table; Mat (Mkeka); Straw Baskets; Plastic Fruits and Vegatables; Basket of Corn (Mazao), Represents children; 2 Clip Boards (For Director and Minda, Optional); Whistle (For director and Minda, Optional); Candleholder (Kinara- Make of wood with seven (7) inserts for Candles); Seven Candles (Mishumaa Saba - One Black, 3 Green, 3 Red); Wooden cup or goblet(For Libation); 10-12 wrapped gifts (Books, mirrors, paper, pens); Drums (Can Be Made By Students; Beads (For Storyteller); Water pot (For Woman). Sun represent Creation and Growth. It can be Yellow, Red, or Orange.

Costumes: African Costumes. Bird costume can be a simple headdress.

Songs:

1. "Celebration" - Sung by children as they decorate.

2. "Kinara (Candleholder) and Mishumaa Saba (Seven Principles)" Explains its meaning.

3. "Kwanzaa: Maulana Karenga Saw A Need" - Gives the History of Kwanzaa.

4. "Habari Gani? What Is The Day?" Children Sing Welcome

5. "We Join Hands" Roma leads song, others join in

6. "Seven Candles - Mishumaa Saba" Reframe

7. "Nguza Saba The First Born"

8. "Zawadi - The Gift"

9. "Kwanzaa Means First Fruit

Glossary

Ankn - Statue: Represents life and man; can be displayed, can be red, brown, yellow, red.

Asante; Asante Sana: Thank you. We honor your presence.

Bindera Ya Taifa - The national Flag: Standard, or colors of Black, for the people; Red, continuing the struggle, Green, the Bounty of the Motherland.

Chicago - Has held an annual Kwanzaa since 1969, in its annual city-wide Karamu Ya Imani.

Habari Gani - What is the news? The answer is one of the Seven Principals.

Harambee – "Let's pull together"
Karamu - The Feast. This is the time of the feast. The community comes and participates. This is on the sixth day of Kwanzaa, on December 31st.

Imani (Ee Mah Nee) "Faith." The Seventh Principal of Kwanzaa.

Karamu Ya Imani - Annual city wide event in the African Community of Chicago, since 1969, an example for other cities and communities in planning such an event.

Kibunza (Vibunzi) Corn. Ears of corn: The symbol for children; off-springs; the generations and future of a people. The stalk is for the parents or potential parents.

Kikombe (Kee kom bay) Unity, (Kikombe Cha Umoja - Kee Kom Bay Cha Oo Mo Jah) Unity Cup: Promoting the spirit of Oneness. We drink (should be from a wooden cup) and say Harambee (Seven times.)

Kinara - Candleholder. Represents the beginning, the first/ original stalk from which we came. It is a symbol of infinity, never ending.

Kiswahili - Swahili - East African language

Kuchanguza Tena Na Kutoa Ahadi Tena - Reassessment and Recommitment

Kujichagulia (Koo Goo Chah Goo Lee Ah) is Self-Determination; the second Principal of Kwanzaa.

Kushangilia - Rejoicing

Kukaribisha - (Welcoming) All guests, elders, are acknowledged and greeted

Kuumba - (Creativity) The 6th value and Principal. Encourages you to always do as much as you can, in every way you can, and to elevate and leave the community better than you found it. It is the Sixth Principal of Kwanzaa.

Kwanzaa - Means first. It links life and times of African Americans in American with the past in Africa. Combines Afro Caribbean, Latin, and African-American customs and ways

Matunda Ya Kwanzaa - First Fruits

Dr. Maulana "Ron" Karenga - Founder of Kwanzaa

Mazao (Mah zah o) "Straw basket:" The Symbol of our roots and Bounty of our labor.

Mishumaa Saba: Mishummaa: (Mee shoo mah Sah bah) - Seven Candles. The Symbol of our ancestors who began and set the order of our society for its best use

Mkeka - Place Mat: The symbol of the foundation of our traditions and history

Muhindi (Moo heen dee) Ears of Corn; Symbol of our Children.

Nia (Nee Ah) Purpose: The Fifth Principal of Kwanzaa.

Ngoma: Drum

Nguzo Saba: Seven Kwanzaa Principles.

Tambika: Libation/Tamshi la Tambiko: Libation or Farewell Statement; a symbol of respect for the ancestors.

Ujamaa (Oo Jah Mah): Co-operative Economics: The fourth Principal of Kwanzaa.

Ujima (Oo Jee Mah): Collective Work and Responsibility. The third Principal of Kwanzaa.

Umoja – Unity: The First Principal. The First Day of Kwanzaa, in family, community, nation, and race.

Watoto (Wah Toh Toh); Our Children

Zawadi (Zah Wah Dee): Gifts. Should be affordable, educational, artistic, natural, handmade i.e., books, candles, poems.

Sources

It's Kwanzaa Time by Linda and Clay Gross, G.P. Putnam and Sons, New York.

Kwanzaa, Everything You Always Wanted To Know But Didn't Know Where To Ask, (Revised Edition), Cedric McClester, Gumbs and Thomas Publishers, New York.

Kwanzaa, A progressive and Uplifting African-American Holiday, Haki R. Madhobuti, Third World Press, Chicago.

Other Cheudi Publications

Life Lessons, Henry O. Adkins

After The Beginning In The Garden, Sue L. Adkins

Raising Great Kids, Henry and Sue L. Adkins

Kwanzaa Celebration, Sue L. Adkins

Out of The Corner Of My Eye, Sue L. Adkins

StringTown, Sue L. Adkins

My Bible ABC's, Henry O. Adkins

KWANZAA CELEBRATION

Children/Play

"Kwanzaa Celebration" is a play which focuses on a group of children at a community center who hosts a Kwanzaa event. Tension and uncertainty develops over whether the event will go on as planned. The Swahili language is used to introduce the principles and symbols to build and strengthen people, families and communities. You are invited to learn and enjoy the celebration through the language, songs, dance, and stories which come together in a rich and vibrant message of oneness.

Sue L. Adkins writes fiction and children's plays and books. She lives with her family in Plano Texas and works with her church, bringing productions of her work and the work of other writers to the congregation. Sue shares a message of hope and enlightenment in this text and introduces you to a positive cultural experience. She encourages groups and organizations to perform this work in celebration of the blended customs and traditions of a people.

ISBN 0-9672605-3-1
Cheudi Publishing
P.O. Box 940572
Plano, Texas 75094-0572

Made in the USA
Coppell, TX
20 December 2020